MW00874103

If found please return to:

Made in the USA
Las Vegas, NV
24 October 2020

10304592R00063